Raise the Bar
Initial to Grade 2

Piano

Teaching Notes written by Graham Fitch

Published by
Trinity College London Press
www.trinitycollege.com

Registered in England
Company no. 09726123

Copyright © 2016 Trinity College London Press
Second impression, November 2021

Unauthorised photocopying is illegal
No part of this publication may be copied or reproduced in any
form or by any means without the prior permission of the publisher.

Printed in England by Caligraving Ltd.

Contents

Initial
Teaching Notes ... 3
Miaou, Miaou (Mani) ... 5
The Sleeping Doll (Akimov) ... 6
Little Snow-bearing Clouds (Garścia) ... 7
Roundabout (Wright) ... 8
Silent Movie (Sebba) ... 9
Wotcha Doin'? (Sebba) ... 10
Airs and Graces (Sebba) ... 11
Poco allegro (Hässler) ... 12
Children's Dance (Kodály) ... 13
A Porcupine Dance (Kabalevsky) ... 14
Enroulez le fil (Wind the bobbin up) (Trad. French) ... 15
The Little Dove (Trad. Czech) ... 16

Grade 1
Teaching Notes ... 17
Allegretto in C (Diabelli) ... 18
Mélodie (le Couppey) ... 19
Dance (Goedicke) ... 20
Safe Landing (Maxwell Davies) ... 21
Reggae (Norton) ... 22
Courante (Greenidge) ... 23

Grade 2
Teaching Notes ... 24
Minuet (Sheeles) ... 25
Allegro in G (L Mozart) ... 26
Waltz (Clementi) ... 28
Jack Tar (Rowley) ... 29
King's Cross (Williamson) ... 30
The Sparrow (Lvov-Kompaneets) ... 31

Teaching Notes – Initial

Miaou, Miaou (Mani)

Two cats call to each other; the left hand answering the right. Start off softly, but make the second phrase (bar 5) softer still. The last phrase (from the end of bar 8) begins more firmly (*mf*), but this time the LH answers with an echo (*mp*). The music now fades away, and our two cats fall asleep together (notice the **rit.** at the end). The piece is in the key of A minor, but finishes in the major – enjoy the warmth of the LH C♯ in the last chord.

Play the slurred pairs carefully (the second note lighter than the first) and aim for a beautiful *legato cantabile* in the RH when both hands play together. The dynamic levels should be the same in both hands in bars 1 and 2, but when the RH has the melody (bars 3 and 4, 7 and 8, etc) it needs to be played more strongly than the LH.

The Sleeping Doll (Akimov)

This gentle piece serves as a study in co-ordination between the hands, which are both in the treble clef and above middle C. There are four two-bar phrases; the first and the third are identical.

The LH provides a softly rocking accompaniment to the RH melody, which needs to be beautifully shaped in a singing style (you'll find the right way to do this if you first sing the melody once or twice). We make a very slight gap at the ends of the RH phrases so the music can breathe. It is important to maintain the *legato* in the LH between bars 1 and 2, 3 and 4 etc. Did you spot that every other LH note is D (played with the 4th finger), apart from the last bar when the LH joins the RH on the key note?

Little Snow-bearing Clouds (Garścia)

This imaginative piece is in two sections, divided by the double bar line; both sections are identical apart from the dynamics (*forte* in the first section, *piano* in the second). Pay careful attention to phrase shaping in both loud and soft playing by tapering the sound at the end of the short and long phrases, and making a tiny break in the *legato*.

Even though there is no key signature, we feel the key as D minor. There is one note that doesn't belong in the key, the E♭ in bars 8 and 16. This chromatic note takes us by surprise and adds a dark colour to the phrase ending. The bare fifth that follows in both hands adds to the bleak mood, and we know snow is on its way.

Roundabout (Wright)

There is a joyful feeling of spinning in this exciting piece. If you play it fast enough you will certainly imagine you are on a roundabout, but it is a good plan to practise slowly and deliberately at first.

In the opening phrase, make sure the bouncy *staccato* crotchets match in touch and dynamics as you pass them back and forth between the hands. The LH must be just as good as the RH! From bar 6 we have short slurred groups, and a sudden *diminuendo* to *p*. Play the syncopated *tenuto* minims in the LH firmly within the soft dynamic, both notes sounding precisely together. Make a small break at the end of each slur, even when this note is a minim (bars 7, 8, etc). Do you like a slight slowing down at the end, or do you think the tempo should stay the same? It can work well either way.

Silent Movie (Sebba)

In the early days of cinema before sound, a pianist might improvise music to help tell the story as the silent movie played on the screen. What is going on in this scene, do you think?

There are two contrasting ideas – a *ff* statement with both hands playing the same notes an octave apart, and a *pp* answer in chords (this design changes in the last phrase). Both ideas feature syncopation (a shift of accent occurring when a normally weak beat is stressed). Playing syncopations might cause the tempo to wobble, so it is very important to feel a steady pulse throughout. A metronome can help, or you might count out aloud as you practise. Make as big a difference as you can between the *ff* and the *pp* dynamics. Your chords will sound better if you can make the top note of each one slightly stronger than the notes below.

Wotcha Doin'? (Sebba)

In some popular styles such as jazz and swing, the notation of the rhythm is sometimes approximate. In this piece we make the dotted rhythms feel lazy by playing them as triplets. Notice the accents, especially those that come on the off-beats (bars 2, 4, etc) as they help to give the music its cheeky character. Observe all rests – the silences are just as important as the notes here – and enjoy the sudden dynamic contrasts in the last line.

Sometimes the appearance of accidentals in music indicates a change of key; other times extra sharps or flats that don't belong in the key are used to add colour, but without any modulation. The word 'chromatic' comes from the Greek word 'chroma', meaning colour. Some of the additional sharps you see are known as chromatic neighbour tones (bar 1), or passing notes (bar 8).

Airs and Graces (Sebba)

This elegant piece is a polite conversation between the two hands. In the first four bars the RH decorates an ascending five-finger position in flowing quaver motion; the LH descends in a dotted rhythm. In bars 5 and 6 the LH imitates the quaver movement. Notice the *crescendo* in the first ending. The repeat is an important structural element of this piece giving us the opportunity to play *p* first time and *f* the second time.

Release the LH minim notes precisely in bars 1 and 2 – the 5th finger comes up exactly as the RH 3rd finger plays the B. Even though these are not marked, it is fine for us to add *crescendo* and *diminuendo* to make the lines expressive. Try making a small *crescendo* in the ascending patterns, and a small *diminuendo* in the descending ones.

Poco allegro (Hässler)

The form of the piece is ternary (ABA), the repeat of the A section indicated by a **da capo** and the ending with **Fine**. Notice the modulation to the dominant key of G towards the end of the B section.

The mood is bright but don't rush. A steady tempo will help you to master the main challenge of this piece, how to change back and forth from duplet to triplet quavers while keeping each quaver group even and the underlying crotchet pulse rock-steady. This is a skill all musicians need to master. It will help to start by clapping crotchets while saying words out loud that fit with the patterns the RH has to play – such as 'ap-ple' for the duplet quavers, and 'straw-ber-ry' for the triplets.

Children's Dance (Kodály)

Zoltán Kodály was a Hungarian composer and educator who developed his own approach to teaching, known as the Kodály Method. The pentatonic scale features quite a lot in his music; you can find it easily by playing the black notes on the piano. This scale has only 5 notes, and no semitones (do, re, mi, so, la).

In *Children's Dance*, the LH plays fifths (with 1 and 5) and then thirds (with 2 and 4) in a steady stream of quavers in the manner of drum beats. Keep the quavers bouncy and *staccato*. The RH has some *staccato* notes too, but also some slurred groups. Make the last note of each group short. In order to manage the constant shifts in hand position, it is important to play with a free and supple wrist. This piece could also be approached by playing each note up a semitone on the black keys.

A Porcupine Dance (Kabalevsky)

Dmitri Kabalevsky was a Russian composer who wrote a lot of music for children and developing pianists. *A Porcupine Dance* is a very effective piece, built from broken triads moving in contrary motion between the hands.

It will be much easier to learn this piece if you notice there are only three different hand positions, laid out in the first three bars. It might be helpful at first to practise all of the notes in each position together as a block chord so you can feel how one hand fits with the other. Can you feel the two thumbs sitting together on adjacent notes? Play all quavers short and bouncy, and enjoy the spiky accents. Watch out for the sudden drop to *p* in bar 9, and the gradual *crescendo* back to *mf*. The accents disappear here for a while, but return on the last three notes.

Enroulez le fil (Wind the bobbin up) (Traditional French)

This arrangement of a traditional French song is an excellent study in singing tone, combining delicate touches and independence between the hands. The RH is in C major five-finger position throughout, but the LH moves around more and has plenty to do. Begin by singing the melody – to 'la' if you don't know the words.

The first two phrases are identical in notes and rhythm – aim for a clear dynamic contrast between *p* and *f*. Observe the rests precisely in the RH of bars 3 and 7 without them affecting the smooth and even LH scale pattern. Watch out also for the rests in both hands at the end of the phrases; these allow the music to breathe. The last phrase poses two challenges: playing *staccato* in one hand while playing *legato* in the other, and controlling the short slurs without losing co-ordination between the hands.

The Little Dove (Traditional Czech)

This traditional Czech song is a little study in scale patterns and broken chords. It is in the key of C major with chromatic harmonies in the last phrase that add colour and interest. The time signature of $\frac{2}{2}$ (alla breve) tells us to feel two minim beats in each bar.

The tune is repeated twice; exactly the same in the RH, but the LH is different the second time. In the first phrase, the LH plays a one-octave descending scale of C in minims; in the second phrase the LH is rather more active. How do bars 3 and 4 differ from bars 7 and 8? Practise the LH broken major triads from bar 7 as solid triads before you break them up as written. It also helps if you can name them.

Miaou, Miaou

Jacqueline Mani

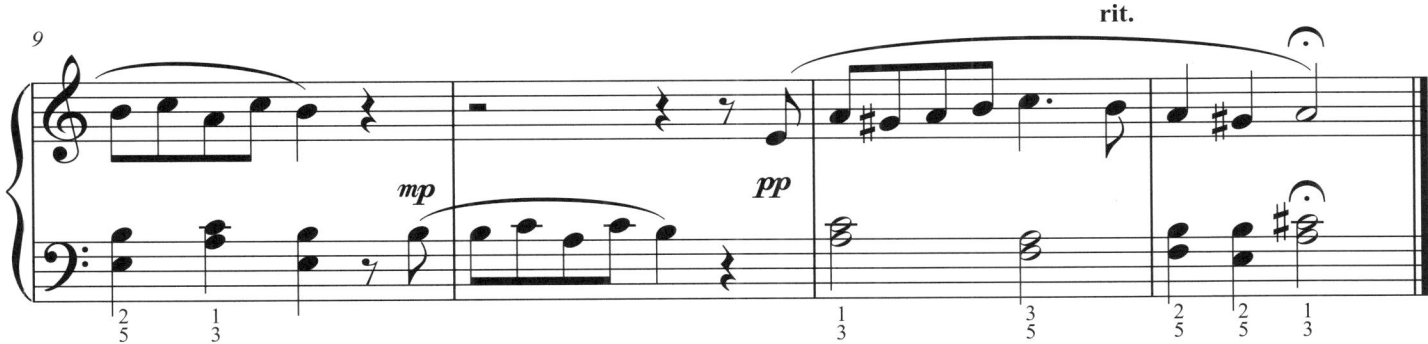

Copyright © by Jacqueline Mani.

Initial

The Sleeping Doll

K Akimov

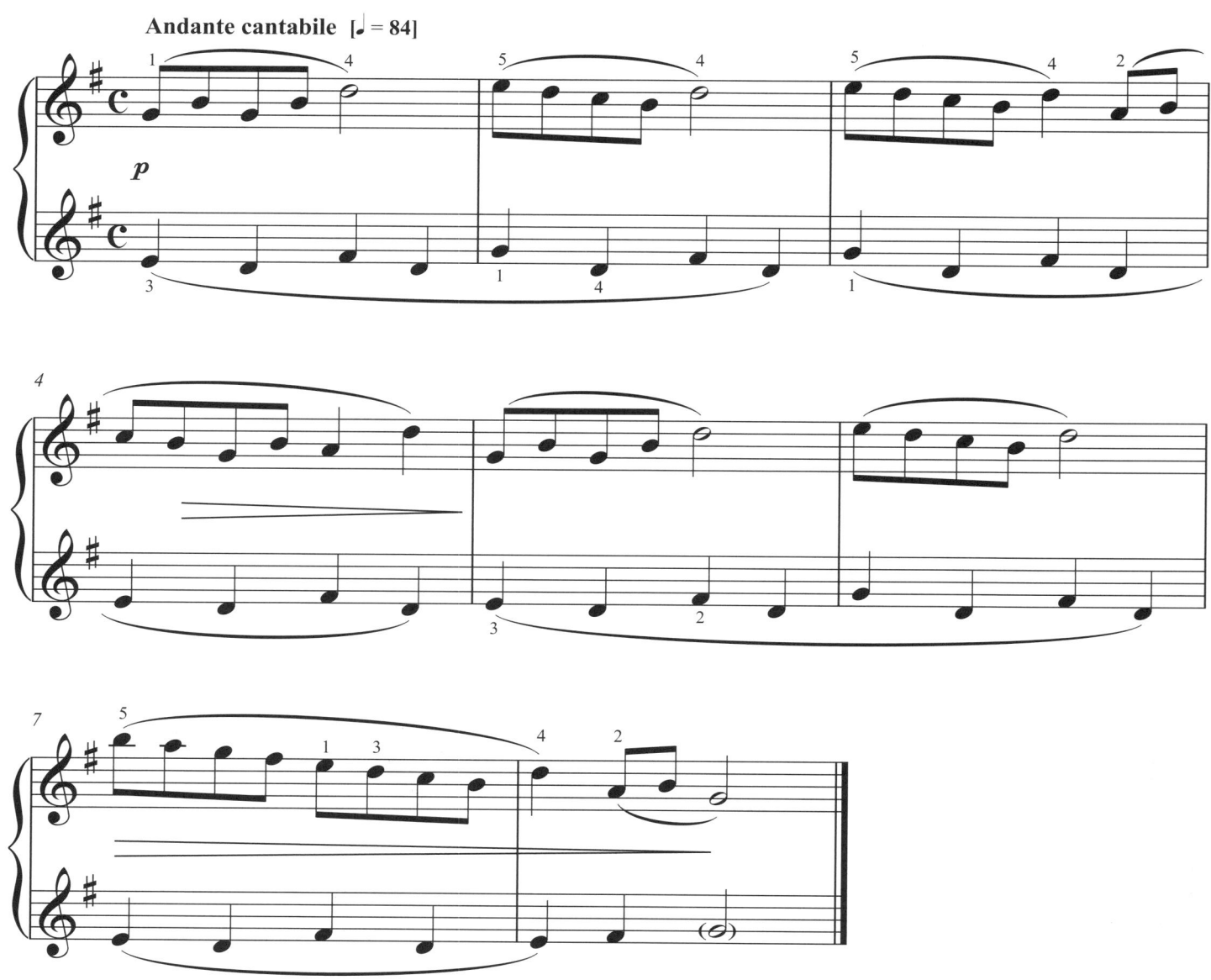

Initial

Little Snow-bearing Clouds

op. 21

Janina Garścia
(1920–2004)

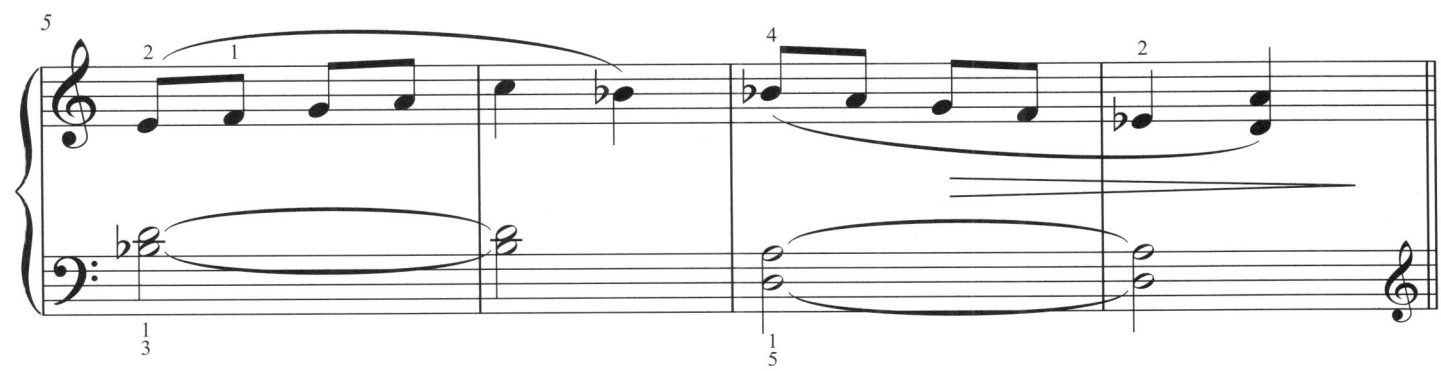

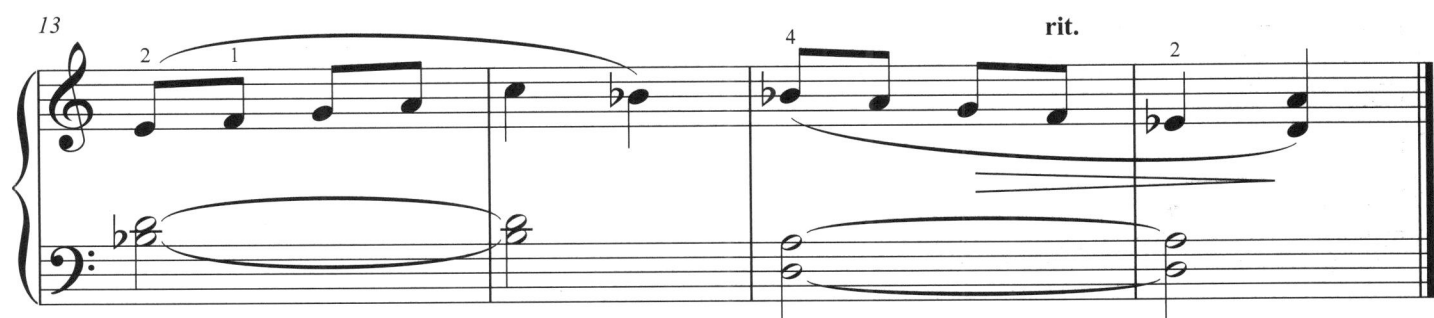

Copyright © 1956 by Polskie Wydawnictwo Muzyczne SA, Kraków, Poland.
All rights reserved.

Initial

Roundabout

David Wright
(b. 1931)

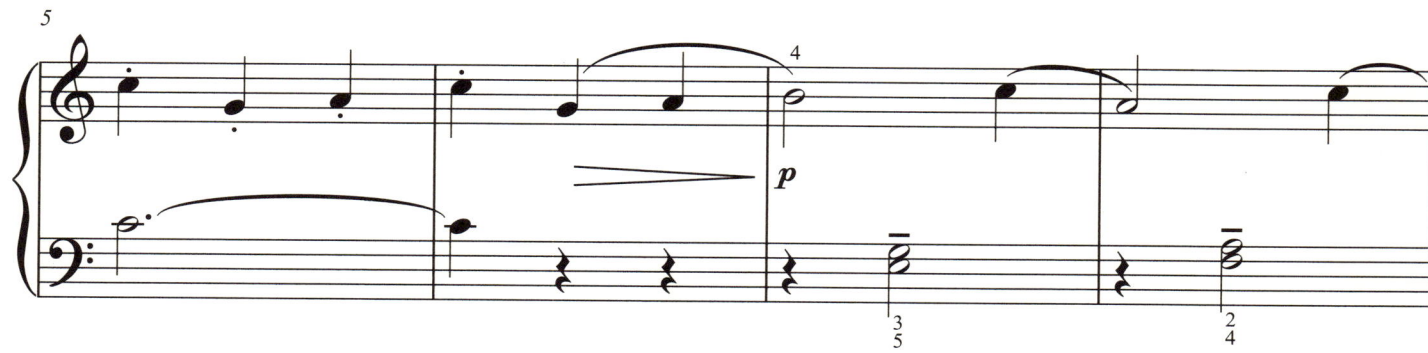

Copyright © 2000 by David Wright.

Initial

Silent Movie

Jane Sebba
(b. 1956)

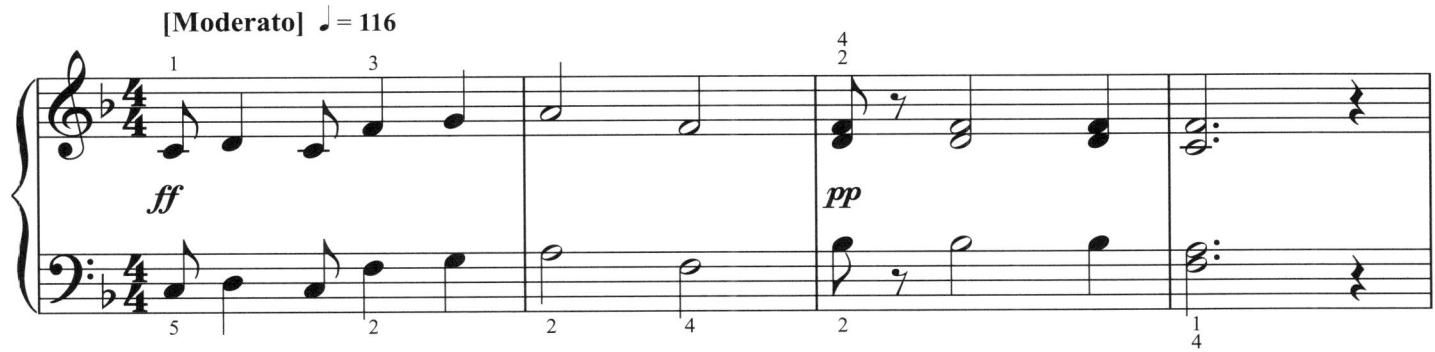
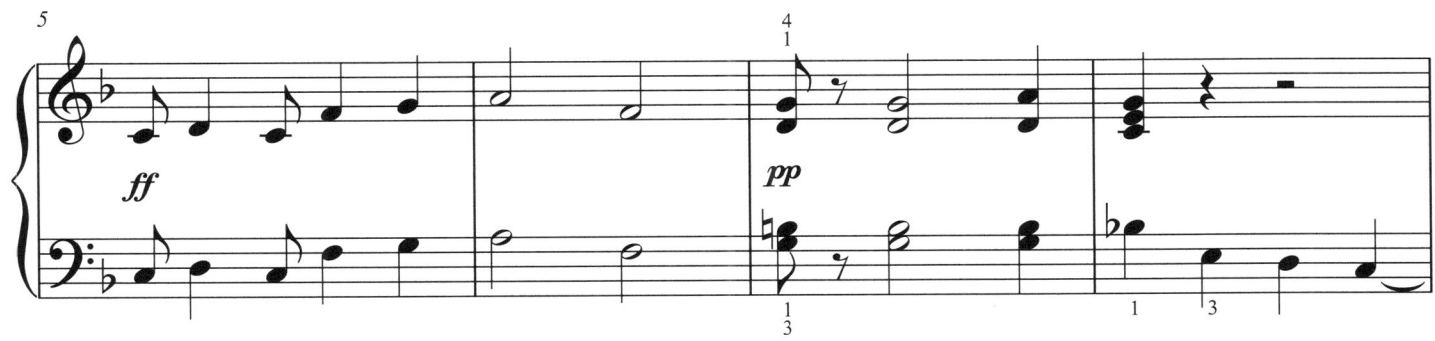
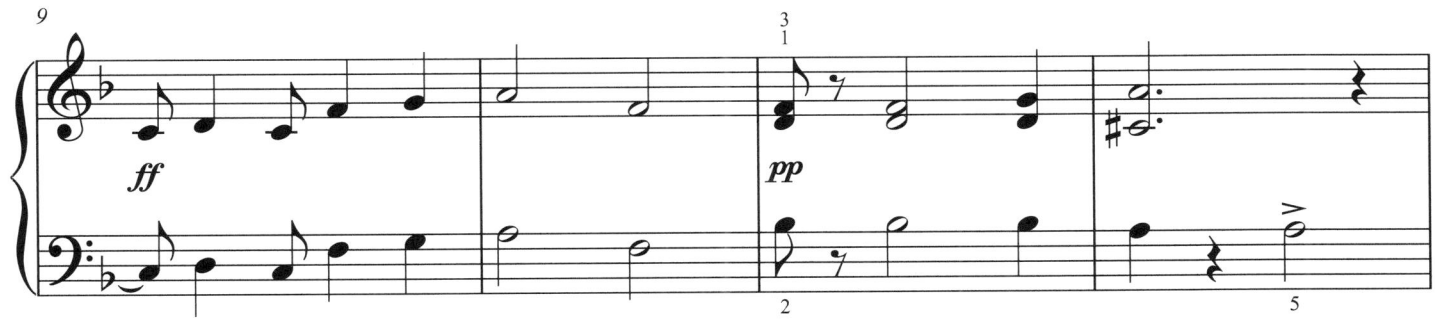

Copyright © 1995 by Jane Sebba.

Initial

Wotcha Doin'?

Jane Sebba
(b. 1956)

Initial

Airs and Graces

Jane Sebba
(b. 1956)

Poco allegro

from *50 Pieces for Beginners*, op. 38, no. 2

Johann Wilhelm Hässler
(1747-1822)

Cheerfully [♩ = 80]

Initial

Children's Dance

Zoltán Kodály
(1882-1967)

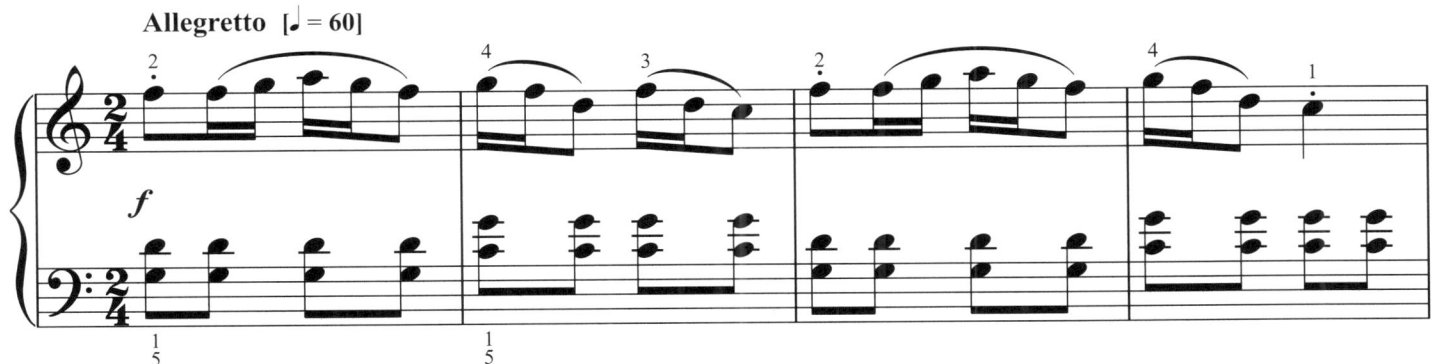

Copyright © 1947 by Hawkes & Son (London) Ltd.

A Porcupine Dance

Dmitri Kabalevsky
(1904-1987)

Copyright © 1978 by Boosey & Hawkes Music Publishers Ltd;
for the United Kingdom, British Commonwealth (ex. Canada) and South Africa.

Initial

Enroulez le fil
(Wind the bobbin up)

Arr. Jane Sebba

Traditional French

Copyright © 1995 by Jane Sebba.

Initial

The Little Dove

Traditional Czech

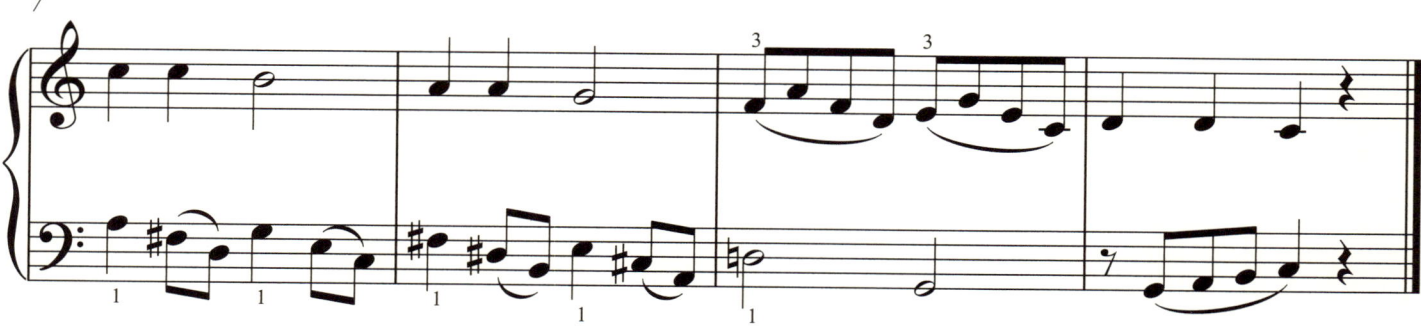

Copyright © 2000 by Trinity College London.

Teaching Notes – Grade 1

Allegretto in C (Diabelli)

The character of this Allegretto is cheerful and buoyant, but don't take it too fast (*allegretto* is slower than *allegro* but faster than *andante*). Listen carefully to the balance between the hands; the RH melody must always sing out above the LH accompaniment. Aim to play the accents (bars 1, 5, etc) more strongly than the *tenutos* (bars 2, 6, etc). *Tenutos* are not as distinct; they just need to be given a little more weight. Observe the *diminuendo* in bars 4 and 8 and play the quavers lightly and delicately. Acciaccaturas (bars 3 and 19) are best played together with the main note, very lightly.

Be careful not to rush after the double bar when the music changes. The LH now plays smoothly but the tempo should stay exactly the same.

Mélodie (le Couppey)

This gentle piece serves as a study in tonal balance between the hands, and in shaping a melodic line. Project the RH melody, imagining perhaps a violin or a flute, and observe the sudden change to *pp* in bar 7. Play the LH accompaniment lightly, smoothly and evenly. You might learn the LH broken chords by first playing them as solid triads (a practice technique known as 'blocking'). This helps you feel the different chord shapes as the harmonies change.

The B section (bars 9-16) is in the subdominant key (F major). Notice that the LH is now playing solid chords, and that the lowest note is always F even when the harmony changes (eg bar 10).

Dance (Goedicke)

A strong rhythmic pulse and careful grading of dynamic levels are necessary for a successful performance of this playful dance. Play the *staccato* notes crisply and the quavers evenly, holding the minims for their full value. Ensure that chords are placed firmly and listen for all notes sounding together.

This 16-bar piece in E minor has four phrases; the first one repeated three times but with two differences. Notice that the RH in bar 8 is a slightly decorated version of bar 4, and that the last phrase (starting in bar 13) is *f* (instead of *mf*). The third phrase (from bar 9) starts *p* – as you build the *crescendo* see if you can do so gradually rather than all at once.

Safe Landing (Maxwell Davies)

Peter Maxwell Davies lives on the remote Orkney Islands off the north coast of Great Britain. *Safe Landing* is the third piece in the set 'Stevie's Ferry to Hoy', and is a beautiful picture in sound.

The tempo indication is **Andante**; flowing but unhurried. The RH sets the scene with the repeated notes, marked *pp* and *staccato*. Play them drily with no sense of hurry (repeated notes do have a tendency to rush). The LH has the melody line throughout – play it firmly but very expressively, observing the slurs and *staccato* notes. The time signature changes back and forth from $\frac{4}{4}$ to $\frac{2}{4}$, with a $\frac{5}{4}$ bar near the end. There is a little touch of uncertainty here – perhaps Stevie hesitates before he hops off the ferry onto dry land? Be very careful to count this odd bar correctly, and enjoy the moment.

Reggae (Norton)

Reggae is a genre of music that originated in Jamaica in the 1960s, influenced by jazz, rhythm and blues and calypso music.

The RH has syncopated stresses on the (usually weak) second and fourth beats. Play the RH chords not *staccato* but *tenuto* – holding them for the full crotchet value. This piece uses the primary triads (chords I, IV and V), but there are two bars that feature chord vi (a minor chord). Can you find them? The LH melody needs to be firmly projected at the given dynamic levels. Be careful not to rush the triplet crotchets in the LH (bars 8, 20, etc); these notes need to be evenly spaced.

Courante (Greenidge)

A courante is a dance in triple time, lively in character. This courante from the modern era is in baroque style, both hands equally important (like a duo between a violin and cello).

A strong sense of rhythm is needed in order to bring out the dance quality in this piece. Give the RH minims in bars 2, 4 and 8 a little more weight (*tenuto*), and put the stress on the first note of the LH slurs that cross the bar line (bars 9 and 10, 10 and 11 etc). Lighten the second note, even though this note falls on the downbeat. There are very few marks of expression, meaning you can add some of your own. Do you sense where you might want to include *crescendo* and *diminuendo* effects?

Grade 1

Allegretto in C
op. 125, no. 10

Antonio Diabelli
(1781–1858)

Grade 1

Mélodie

from *ABC du piano*, 1859

Félix le Couppey
(1811-1887)

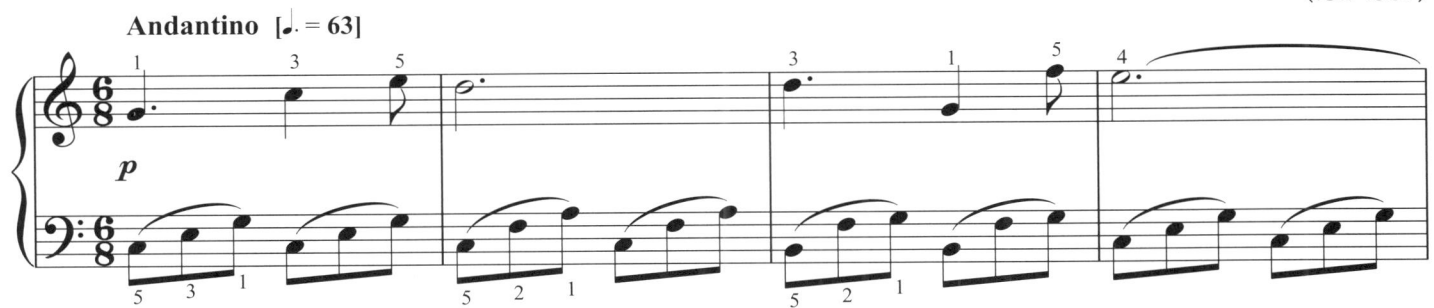

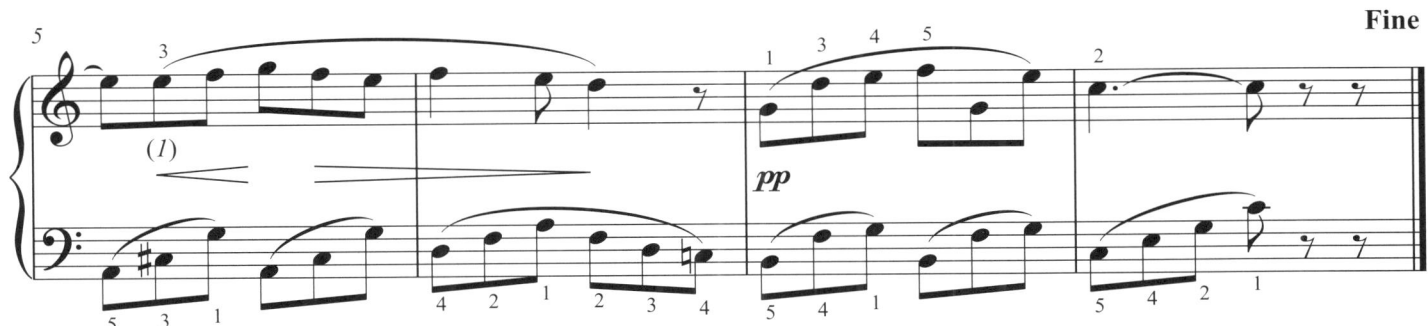

Fingering and left-hand slurring are given according to the Paris edition, 1877.

Original markings: (1) *legato* (2) *legatissimo*

Copyright © 2000 by Trinity College London.

Dance

Alexander Goedicke
(1877-1957)

Safe Landing

Peter Maxwell Davies
(b. 1934)

Copyright © 1978 by Boosey & Hawkes Music Publishers Ltd.

Reggae

Christopher Norton
(b. 1953)

Courante

Rosalind Anne Greenidge
(b. 1957)

Teaching Notes – Grade 2

Minuet (Sheeles)

This minuet by John Sheeles is from his suite of dance movements in the key of A major, written for the harpsichord or spinet around 1725. You might want to research the sounds of these instruments. To bring out the graceful dance character of the minuet, play the first beat of the bar a little more strongly than the second and third beats.

In line with standard practice of the day, Sheeles marked no performance directions in the score at all, leaving the choice of articulation and dynamics to the good taste of the performer. The slurs, phrase markings, dynamic markings and *staccatos* here are editorial. They are suggestions only and are included to help you add colour and contrast to your performances. They do represent the types of articulation that would have been used by performers in this period.

Allegro in G (L Mozart)

Leopold Mozart was responsible for the early musical training of his two children, Wolfgang Amadeus and Nannerl. The *Allegro in G* comes from a book of short pieces and exercises he compiled for his daughter, entitled 'Notebook for Nannerl'.

Apart from some short slurs and phrase marks that indicate *legato*, many performance decisions have been left to the player. Think of the LH as your conductor, and play the unmarked quavers non-*legato* (firmly and not too short). RH semiquavers should be clearly articulated and very even in touch. The RH slurred pairs call for an expressive approach, the first note strong and the second note weaker and slightly shorter than marked. A *crescendo* helps to bring shape to ascending sequences (bars 5-8 and 39-43). The section in the relative minor (bars 27-34) needs a new colour, and might be played more delicately.

Waltz (Clementi)

Muzio Clementi was an Italian composer, pianist, music publisher and piano manufacturer who settled in London in 1774.

Feeling one beat in a bar (rather than three) will help prevent this charming waltz in E flat major from becoming laboured, as will good tonal balance between the hands. Listen carefully that the LH repeated notes do not cover the RH melody, which needs to be played with projection and attention to the composer's articulation markings. Play the LH at least one, or possibly two dynamic notches less than the RH (thus RH *f*, LH *mf* or *mp*). The *Waltz* is built up of 8-bar phrases throughout, and is in two halves. In order to finish in the home key, Clementi reorganises the material in the second half. Can you see how he has done it?

Jack Tar (Rowley)

Jack Tar was once a common term for a sailor, and this piece is his dance – a jolly hornpipe in C major. There are two main technical demands the player must meet. In the RH, ensure evenness between the 5th and 4th fingers in the opening figure whenever it recurs at three distinct dynamic levels (*mf*, *f* and *mp*). In the LH, attend to precision in the *legato* double thirds, listening that both notes sound together.

There are two opportunities to broaden the tempo – the **allargando** at the end and also the descending scale in bars 19-20. When we see *staccato* dots under a phrase mark, we play half way between *legato* and *staccato* – the effect here is like running in dry sand. The fermata (⌒) in bar 20 gives us license to hold the G (and the dominant chord in the LH) for as long as we feel is right.

King's Cross (Williamson)

This jazzy piece is part of a set of pieces called 'Travel Diaries' written in the early 1960s by Australian composer, Malcolm Williamson. *King's Cross* evokes the hustle and bustle of the nightclub district of Sydney.

The piece is built from one type of chord divided up between the two hands – the chord of the added 6th (a major or minor triad with the 6th degree of the scale added to it). Play with the same pair of fingers in each hand throughout (until the last chord, which breaks the pattern). The syncopations will only come to life if the pulse is rock-steady. Clapping the rhythm while counting aloud (firstly crotchet beats and then two-in-a-bar) is excellent practice. Pay careful attention to note lengths and accents.

The Sparrow (Lvov-Kompaneets)

This descriptive piece in C major relies on a lightness of touch and spirit for its effect. Pay careful attention to the articulation markings, making sure to phrase off the slurred groups delicately, and to give emphasis to the *tenuto* crotchets (bars 4, 20, etc).

The piece is in ternary (ABA) form, the B section (bars 9-16) in the dominant key of G major and marked *forte*. The composer has an interesting surprise for us when the A section returns. Several unexpected flats appear in the last phrase, outlining the chord of D flat major (in the key of C major this chord is known as the Neapolitan 6th). What effect does this have on the mood, for you?

Minuet

from *Suite in A*, c.1725

John Sheeles
(early 18th century)

Source: British Library MS, RISM S 2915.
Dynamics and articulation marks are editorial.

Allegro in G

No. 37 from *Notebook for Nannerl*, 1759

Leopold Mozart
(1719-1787)

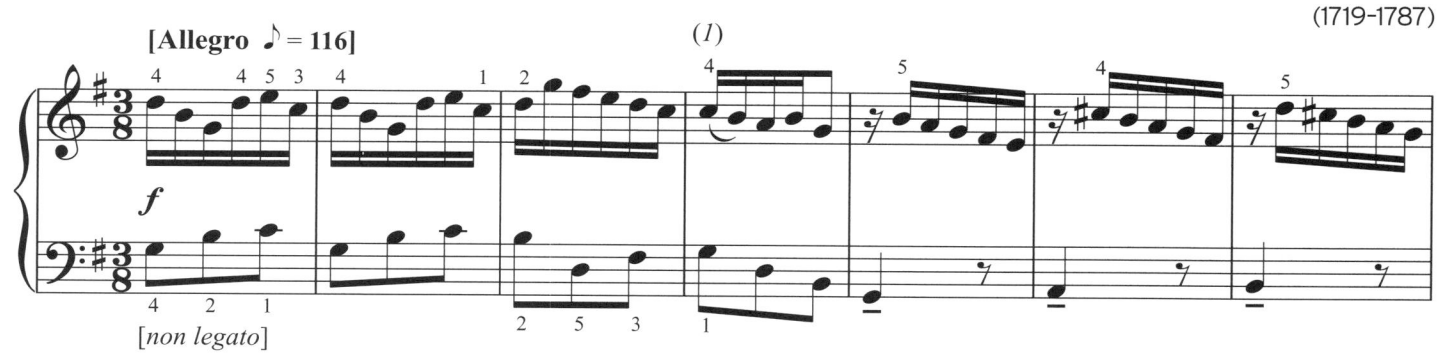

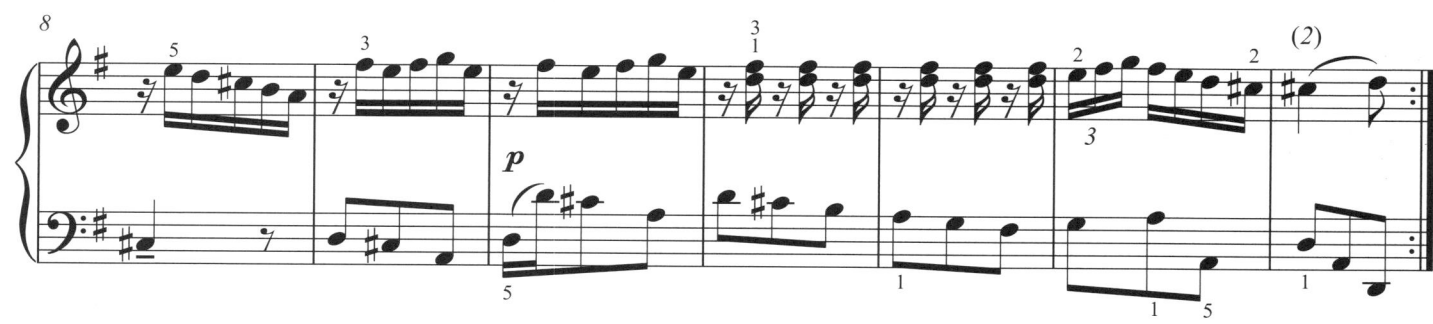

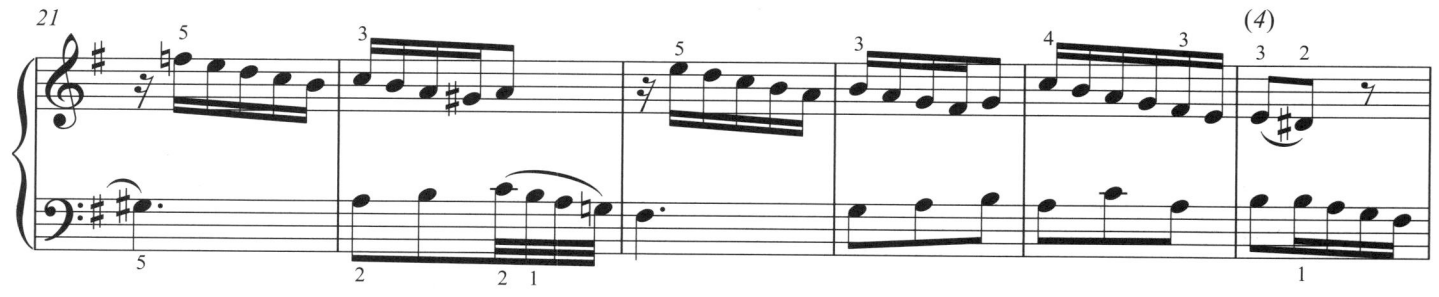

Dynamics and articulation marks are editorial.

Grade 2

Waltz

Muzio Clementi
(1752–1832)

Dynamic marks are editorial.

Jack Tar

Alec Rowley
(1892-1958)

Grade 2

King's Cross

(the Bohemian, cosmopolitan, nightclub district of Sydney)

Malcolm Williamson
(1931-2003)

Copyright © 1987 by Campion Press.
Reprinted from *Travel Diaries* by permission of the copyright owners.

The Sparrow

D Lvov-Kompaneets